EDGE
BOOKS™

Dazzling

Card

Tricks

by Norm Barnhart

CAPSTONE PRESS
a capstone imprint

Edge Books are published by Capstone Press,
1710 Roe Crest Drive, North Mankato, Minnesota 56003
www.capstonepub.com

Library of Congress Cataloging-in-Publication Data
Barnhart, Norm.
Dazzling card tricks / by Norm Barnhart.
pages cm.—(Edge books. Magic manuals)
Includes bibliographical references.
Summary: "Step-by-step instructions and photos show how to do a variety of fun and
entertaining card tricks"—Provided by publisher.
ISBN 978-1-4765-0133-8 (library binding)
ISBN 978-1-4765-3389-6 (ebook PDF)
1. Card tricks—Juvenile literature. I. Title.
GV1549.B315 2014
793.8'5—dc23   2013004918

Editorial Credits
Aaron Sautter, editor; Tracy Davies McCabe, designer; Svetlana Zhurkin,
media researcher; Jennifer Walker, production specialist; Sarah Schuette,
photo stylist; Marcy Morin, photo scheduler

Photo Credits
All interior photos by Capstone Studio/Karon Dubke.
Cover and background images by Shutterstock/Anna Subbotina, argus, prospero,
and Valentin Agapov.

Printed in the United States of America in Stevens Point, Wisconsin.
032013   007227WZF13

TABLE OF CONTENTS

COOL CARD MAGIC

People love watching magicians do seemingly impossible things. But you don't need fancy props and flashy lights to blow people's minds. Criss Angel, David Blaine, and other popular magicians often wow people with nothing more than a simple deck of cards.

There are several types of card tricks. The most common is the "pick a card" trick, in which a magician finds a volunteer's chosen card. In this book you'll learn to find a volunteer's chosen card in several ways. You'll learn cool tricks like making cards appear out of thin air. You'll even learn to make cards seem to appear to float into the air on their own. With practice, you'll soon see your friends' jaws dropping in amazement!

Card Magic Secret: The Forced Card

Many card tricks use a secret method called the Forced Card. Magicians use this method to secretly force someone to pick a pre-chosen card. The card can then be revealed in many amazing ways. If you master this method, you'll astound your audience with several of the tricks found in this book.

1. Place a pre-chosen card face down on top of the deck. When you perform the trick, shuffle the cards. But be sure to keep this special card face down on top of the deck as you shuffle the cards.

2. Ask a volunteer to cut the deck and put the top half on the table.

3. Pick up the bottom half of the deck and set it sideways on the top half. The pre-chosen card will be the top card of the bottom stack. As you do this, distract the volunteer by asking for his or her name. This will keep the volunteer's attention focused on you instead of the cards. Then point to the pre-chosen card on the top of the bottom stack.

4. Next, ask the volunteer to pull out the pre-chosen card, memorize it, and place it back in the deck. The volunteer has now "picked" the card you need. You can then shuffle the deck again and go on with the trick. Perform these steps casually, and volunteers will never realize that they did not really pick the card.

TRICK ONE
Magnetic Attraction

Show your friends your magnetic personality! They'll gasp in amazement when they see regular playing cards defy gravity and stick to your hand.

What You Need:

- a ring
- a toothpick
- several playing cards

PREPARATION:

1. Hide the toothpick in your pocket. When you're ready for the trick, casually place your hand inside your pocket and slip the toothpick under your ring.

PERFORMANCE:

1. Hold up a card and say, "People say I have a magnetic personality. Let me show you why." Smoothly slide a card under the secret toothpick (1a). But keep your hand face down so the audience can't see the toothpick (1b). Keep your fingers straight to snugly hold the card against your hand. Then hold up your hand to show the audience that the card sticks!

2. Add more cards under the toothpick one at a time so they appear to stick to your hand.

3. Ask someone in the audience to snap his or her fingers to break the spell. At that moment bend your fingers slightly to let the cards drop.

4. Pick up the cards and say, "Thanks for making those cards fall off. It would be hard to finish the show with them stuck on my hand!" As you put the cards away, secretly slip off the toothpick and put it with the cards.

The Pirate King

The Pirate King is the incredible, all-knowing card. When someone sticks a knife into the deck, the King will mysteriously predict exactly which card is next to the knife.

What You Need:

- a deck of cards
- a shiny butter knife

PERFORMANCE:

1. Show the king of clubs card and the butter knife to the audience. Tell them, "The incredible Pirate King knows all! He just needs his magical knife to make an amazing prediction."

2. Set the king card to the side and pick up the deck of cards. While holding the cards, ask a volunteer to stick the knife anywhere in the deck.

TIP: To make this trick fun for the audience, try pretending to argue with the king card about which card will be found by the knife.

3. Leave the knife in the deck and set the cards on the table. Next, lift the cards on top of the knife a little. As you do this say, "You could have put the knife anywhere, but you chose this spot." As you are talking, secretly use the knife as a mirror to see the reflection of the card next to it. Place the cards back on the knife.

4. Now bring the king of clubs card to your ear and pretend it whispers something to you. Look at the card and say, "Really? You think you know what card is next to the knife?" Tell the audience which card will be found next to the knife.

5. Finally, lift the cards off the knife and show the bottom card to the crowd. The audience will be surprised to see that the King predicted the correct card!

CELL PHONE FUN

Did you know you can read a friend's mind with your cell phone? Just use your phone to take a "picture" of your friend's thoughts. She'll be speechless when she sees the card she chose on the screen!

What You Need:

- a deck of cards
- a cell phone with a camera

PREPARATION:

1. Use the camera phone to take a close-up picture of the card you will force. Keep the picture on your phone so it is ready to use for this trick.

PERFORMANCE:

1. Ask a volunteer to choose a card from the deck. Use the Forced Card method on page 5 to make the person pick the photographed card. Ask the volunteer to look at the card and show it to the audience, but not to you.

2. Have the volunteer put the card face down on the table. Now hold the phone up to the person's ear and say, "This amazing magic phone can take pictures of your thoughts. Please think about the card you chose." Then take a picture so the person hears the picture snap.

3. Switch the phone's screen to the picture of the card you took earlier. Look at the screen and say, "Wow! That's incredible!" Show the picture to the volunteer and the audience. They will be stunned when they see the chosen card on the phone.

IS your card Bigger?

This trick will both amaze your audience and make them laugh. The first two tries don't work, but in the end you find that a volunteer's card really is bigger!

What You Need:

- large paper bag
- one jumbo king of clubs card (found in most party supply stores)
- deck of cards

PREPARATION:

1. Place the jumbo king card into the paper bag.

PERFORMANCE:

1. Ask a volunteer to pick a card. Use the Forced Card method on page 5 to make the person pick the king of clubs card.

TIP: Make the audience laugh by looking puzzled during the first steps of this trick. Adding fun facial expressions keeps the audience entertained.

2. Ask the volunteer to look at the card and show it to the audience, but not to you. Then have the volunteer place it back in the deck. Shuffle the deck and toss the cards into the paper sack.

3. Tell the audience that you'll find the chosen card in three tries. Reach into the bag and pull out a three or four card. Ask the volunteer, "Is this your card?" When the volunteer says it isn't ask, "Is your card bigger?" The person will say yes.

4. Say, "Let's try it again." Look in the bag and pull out a nine or 10 card. Ask if this is the volunteer's card. When the person says no, ask, "Is your card bigger?" The volunteer will again say the chosen card is bigger.

5. Hold your hand over the bag and say, "OK, this is my last try." Reach into the bag and pull out the jumbo king card. Show it to the audience and say, "You're right! Your card IS bigger!"

MiND READiNG MADNESS

Want to blow your friends' minds? It's easy to do with just a few cards. The audience thinks a volunteer has amazing mental powers, but you know the mysterious secret!

What You Need:

- **four playing cards**
- **a small paper bag**
- **glue**
- **magic wand**
- **eraser**

PREPARATION:

1. Glue two cards face to face. Glue the other two cards back to back. You will have one card with two faces and another with two backs.

2. When the glue is dry, place the two special cards in the paper bag.

> TIP: When performing this trick, always make sure the proper side of the two-faced card faces forward.

PERFORMANCE:

1. Place the bag on the table. Place the magic wand and eraser in front of the bag. Tell the audience, "There are two cards in this bag, the nine of clubs and the ace of diamonds." Take out the two special cards and show the empty bag to the audience.

2. Pick up the two cards and hold them as shown to show the audience the nine of clubs card (2a). Then flip the cards over to show the ace of diamonds (2b). As you flip the cards, slide the back card over at the same time. This motion creates the illusion that the ace and nine are two separate cards.

3. Drop the cards into the bag and shake them a bit. Take out the double-backed card and place it on the table. Then ask for a volunteer to help.

4. Tell the volunteer, "I want you to guess which card is still in the bag. But you need to first pick up the magic wand or the eraser. If you pick up the wand, you will be able to guess the correct card. But if you pick the eraser, you will guess wrong." Ask the volunteer to pick one of the objects and guess which card is still in the bag.

5. Bring out the double-faced card. If the volunteer is holding the magic wand, show the correct side of the card (5a). If the volunteer is holding the eraser, show the wrong side (5b). You can repeat this trick three or four times. The audience will be mystified that the volunteer chooses correctly whenever he or she is holding the wand!

WHERE'S JACK?

Where are the Jack brothers hiding? With a little magic, a volunteer will find the four jack cards in no time!

What You Need:

- a deck of cards
- a shirt with a chest pocket

PREPARATION:

1. Hide the four jack cards in your chest pocket.

PERFORMANCE:

1. Ask a volunteer to help you with this trick. Shuffle the deck of cards and say, "The Jack brothers love to play hide-and-seek. But I bet you can predict where they're hiding."

2. Place the deck of cards in your pocket in front of the four jacks. Then ask the volunteer, "Please pick a number between one and 10."

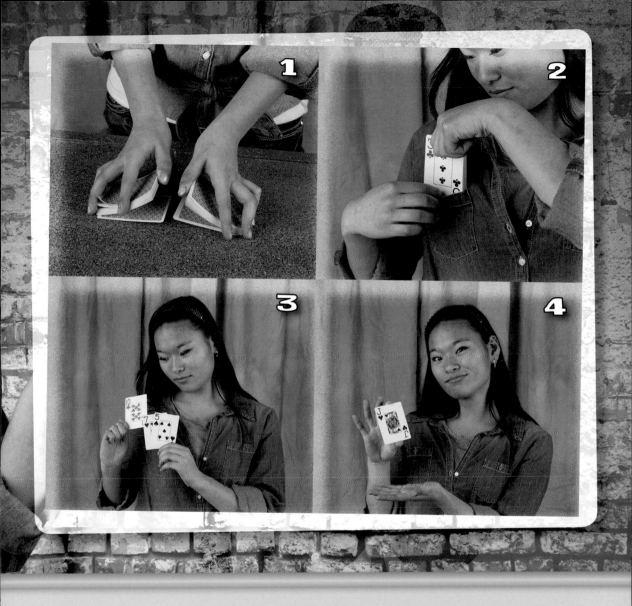

3. Begin counting out loud while pulling cards out one at a time from the front of the deck. When you get to the volunteer's number, pull out a jack from the back of the deck. Hold it up and show the audience. Then say, "You're right! Let's try that again."

4. Repeat the previous step three more times. Each time you get to the volunteer's number, pull out one of the jack cards.

5. When all four jacks have been revealed say, "That was amazing! I knew you had incredible magical powers!" Ask the volunteer to take a bow as the audience cheers.

THE LEVITATING LADY

The Queen of Hearts is a magical lady. Your friends will be astounded when they see her floating at your fingertips!

What You Need:

- clear double-stick tape
- the queen of hearts card

PREPARATION:

1. Place a small piece of double-stick tape on the back of the queen card.

PERFORMANCE:

1. Show the queen of hearts card to the audience. Say, "The Queen of Hearts has an amazing ability. Just snap your fingers and she becomes lighter than air!"

2. Hold the edges of the card with the fingertips of both hands (2a). At the same time, push one thumb against the tape on the back of the card (2b).

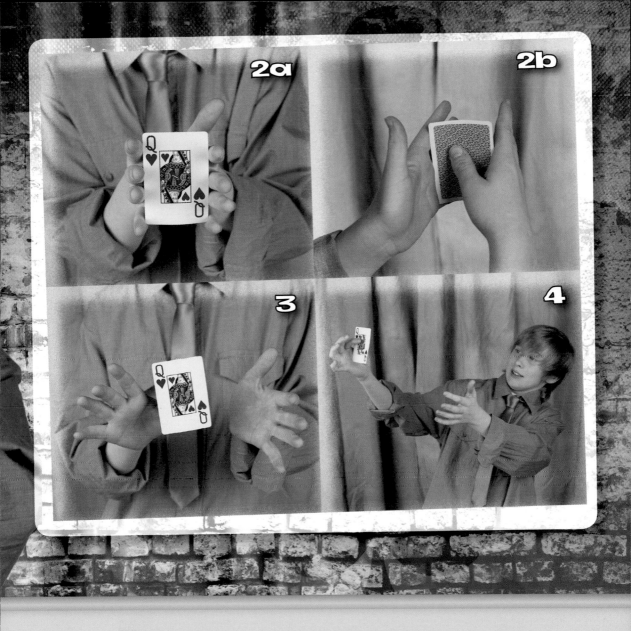

3. Ask the audience to snap their fingers. When they do, release your fingers so the card seems to float in front of your hand. Slowly move your fingers down so the card seems to float up.

4. Move the card up and away from you to pretend that it is floating away. Quickly "catch" the card before it gets away. Give the audience a relieved look and say, "If I don't catch her quick, I won't be playing with a full deck!"

THE IMPOSSIBLE HOLE

Can a large coin travel through a much smaller hole? People will gaze in wonder when you perform this amazing illusion.

What You Need:

- a playing card
- a craft knife
- large coins

PREPARATION:

1. Cut a 1-inch (2.5-centimeter) slit along the white border of a card.

2. Fold the card in half. Then cut a small hole in the center of the fold.

PERFORMANCE:

1. Fold the card in half and place the coin inside. Hold up the card so the audience can see the coin through the hole. Say, "As you can see, the coin can't fit through this tiny hole."

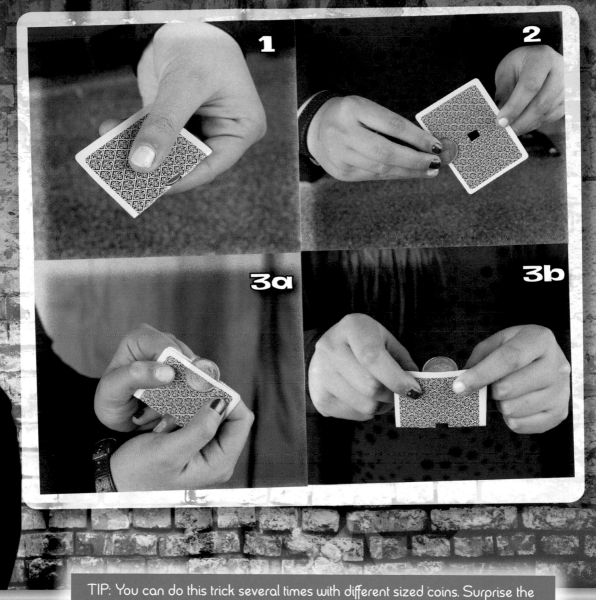

2. Roll the coin out and unfold the card. Hold up the coin and card to show the audience that the coin is bigger than the hole.

3. Tell the crowd, "With a little magic, the coin will slide through the hole right before your eyes!" Fold the card in half again. Place the coin at the top of the card and smoothly slide it through the secret slit (3a). For the audience it will look like you are simply placing the coin inside the card (3b).

4. Slide the coin down the back of the card to cover the hole. Be careful not to slide the coin past the folded edge of the card. Show the audience the coin through the hole. They will think the coin is inside the folded card.

5. Say some magic words like, "Sim Sala Bim!" At the same time, quickly pull the coin away from the card. It will appear to go right through the small hole!

6. Open the card to show the audience that the size of the hole hasn't changed.

Mysterious Rising Card

In this trick a mysterious card appears to come to life! Your friends' jaws will drop when a card rises out of the box on its own.

What You Need:

- **a deck of cards inside a card box**
- **scissors**

PREPARATION:

1. Cut a rectangle in the back of the card box about as wide as your thumb. Make the hole about 2 inches (5 cm) tall.

TIP: You can use almost any mysterious story to grab the audience's attention. Try telling a story about a spooky ghost that likes to assist with your magic tricks.

PERFORMANCE:

1. Fan out the deck of cards and ask a volunteer to pick one.

2. Say, "Please look at the card and show it to your friends. I'll turn around so I can't see it." Turn around after the volunteer picks a card.

3. With your back turned, cut the deck in half and hold the two halves behind your back. Ask the volunteer to place the chosen card on top of the bottom half.

4. Now turn back to face the audience. As you turn, secretly place the bottom half of the deck on top of the top half behind your back. The chosen card is now on top of the deck.

5. Next, place the deck into the card box with the chosen card next to the secret hole. Make sure the volunteer and audience do not see the secret hole.

6. It's time to do some acting. Tell the audience about how you've learned to use the power of your mind. Say, "To prove it, I'll make the volunteer's card rise out of the box!" Hold up the box with your thumb over the secret hole. Hold your other hand next to the box in a dramatic way. Then pretend to concentrate on the chosen card. Slowly push up on the volunteer's card inside the box with your thumb so it appears to rise on its own.

TRICK TEN
THE JUMPING QUEEN

The amazing Queen of Hearts can find any chosen card. She'll stun your friends when she jumps out of the deck to show where a chosen card is hiding.

What You Need:
- **a deck of cards**

PREPARATION:

1. Cut out one corner of the queen of hearts card as shown. Then place the queen on the bottom of the deck.

PERFORMANCE:

1. Fan out the deck and ask a volunteer to pick any card. Don't let the person see the secret queen card on the bottom.

2. Cut the deck into two piles. Ask the volunteer to place the chosen card on the top half of the deck. Then place the bottom half of the deck on the top half. The queen card will now be on top of the volunteer's card.

Volunteer's Card

3. Tell the volunteer about the amazing queen of hearts. Say, "The queen will hop out of the deck if she finds your card." Hold the deck snugly where the corner of the queen is cut out. Use your free hand to start flipping through the cards on the opposite corner.

4. When you get to the queen, it will appear to jump from the deck.

5. Turn the cards over and fan them out. The volunteer's card will be on top of the queen. Pull the card out and ask if it is the volunteer's chosen card. Thank the volunteer and take a bow.

TIP: Don't pull the queen card out or the audience will see the secret that makes the trick work.

crazy card catch

This trick will leave the crowd in awe of your incredible magical powers. The deck of cards is tossed into the air and in a flash the volunteer's card appears in your hand.

What You Need:

- a deck of cards
- two identical ace of spades cards
- very fine thread
- clear tape

PREPARATION:

1. Tape a loop of the thread onto the back of one ace card as shown.

2. Place the secret card into your pants pocket with the loop of thread hanging out.

PERFORMANCE:

1. Ask a volunteer to choose a card from the deck. Use the Forced Card method on page 5 to make the volunteer choose the ace of spades. Ask the volunteer to memorize the card. Then have the volunteer place it back into the deck and shuffle the cards.

2. As the volunteer shuffles the cards, casually place your hand in your pants pocket. Place your thumb through the loop of thread and hide the secret ace in your hand.

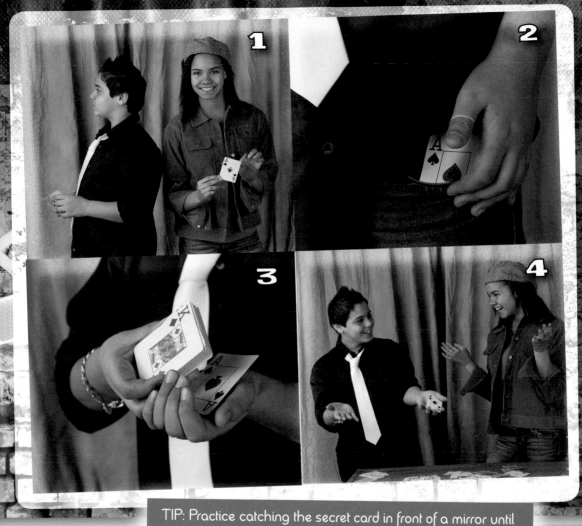

TIP: Practice catching the secret card in front of a mirror until it looks like it magically appears. Keep the back of your hand toward the audience as you make the catching motion.

3. Now ask the volunteer to divide the cards and give you half of them. Take the cards with your free hand and place them over the secret ace in your other hand. Do this quickly and smoothly so the volunteer does not see the secret ace card.

4. Tell the volunteer, "I'll count to three and then we'll both toss our cards into the air." When the cards are tossed, reach up with the hand holding the secret ace and pretend to grab a card out of the air. At the same time, flip the secret ace up between your thumb and finger. Show the volunteer and audience the ace. It will appear that you grabbed the volunteer's card right out of the air!

READ MORE

Fullman, Joe. *Card Tricks.* Magic Handbook. Buffalo, N.Y.: Firefly Books, 2009.

Lane, Mike. *Card Magic.* Miraculous Magic Tricks. New York: Windmill Books, 2012.

Turnbull, Stephanie. *Card Tricks.* Secrets of Magic. Mankato, Minn.: Smart Apple Media, 2012.

INTERNET SITES

FactHound offers a safe, fun way to find Internet sites related to this book. All of the sites on FactHound have been researched by our staff.

Here's all you do:

Visit *www.facthound.com*

Type in this code: 9781476501338

 **Super-cool stuff!** Check out projects, games and lots more at **www.capstonekids.com**